Your Plan for Success

A step-by-step guide to create the life you are meant to live

By Ron Engeldinger

Ron Engeldinger
Visit my website at www.DrRonengeldinger.com

Printed in the United States of America

First Printing: May 2018

ISBN 9781981050086

This book is dedicated to my family; my wife Joan, for everything you do; my sons, Nick and Noah, for your support and encouragement; and my granddaughters Natasha and Kaileigha, who continually inspire me.

CONTENTS

INTRODUCTION

In today's world, getting ahead and making the most out of the path you are on is harder than ever. As the baby boomer generation retires, younger generations are being required to step forward and take leadership roles, and many feel they have not been given the training they need to succeed. Do you know what it takes to become successful in your endeavors? Do you know how to confidently take control of your future?

This is the book that gives you a step-by-step blueprint for personal growth and success. Your Plan for Success has been designed to give you the tools you need to move forward in your life. This book will answer your questions in a straightforward manner and an easy to read style. It will give you the tools that will enable you to confidently move forward toward the life you are meant to live.

With many years of experience as an effective leader and an academic career studying what makes people successful, I have learned what it takes to get ahead in any organization. I learned that a well-crafted plan and an organized approach sets individuals up for achieving their dreams. As a teacher and consultant, both in the U.S. and abroad, I have nurtured thousands of students of all ages as they became successful in their personal and professional endeavors.

I will share the insights that I gained through my own success as I moved up the career ladder and through my experiences as I developed the future leaders in my organization. My goal is to reveal what I have learned so that you will be prepared to meet the challenge and guide yourself on the road to success.

Many people have taken control of their lives and began achieving their goals by following the process found in this helpful guide. Whether you are just beginning your life's journey, or you feel stuck in your current situation, the tools I offer will lead you on a path to success. If you know that you want more out of life but aren't sure what you want, the action steps in this book will help you clarify your current situation and lead you to discover how to go about creating the future you deserve.

The process I describe in this book has provided me with the groundwork for success in my life and my work. I progressed from an inexperienced employee to managerial positions. I ultimately achieved positions of authority and was responsible for overseeing hundreds of employees. I guided the development of my employees and set them up on their own path to success.

You can create a successful life just as my student Susan did. She turned her passion for clothes into a fruitful career in one of the nation's largest fashion retailers. Or, you can blaze your own trail like I did when I uncovered a passion for writing and teaching that I had been ignoring. That discovery led me to walk away from a successful business career and to a focus on helping others achieve their dreams.

I promise that when you follow the step-by-step process, you'll be prepared to move forward in your personal life and your career. You will uncover what you really want out of life. You will position yourself for greater successes in your endeavors. More and better career options will open up to you because you will have the framework and skills to succeed wherever you go. You will achieve greater satisfaction, overcome challenges, and gain recognition for your contributions.

Don't miss out on the opportunities that await you because you lack a plan, and because you don't know what steps you need to take. Become the type of person who takes charge of their life rather than letting life happen to them. Be the kind of person who develops a plan and takes action on that plan. Be the kind of person who others see and say "I want to thrive like they do."

When you don't have a solid plan to reach your goals, it is impossible to know what steps you need to take next, and achieving your goals will always seem to be just out of reach. Be the kind of person who takes positive action to move forward in your life. Take the first step that will lead you on an amazing journey.

The tips for success that you are about to read have been proven to create long-lasting results allowing you to take control of your life and career. Every chapter will give you a new understanding of how you can achieve greater success in your life and work. This book gives you detailed action steps that will take you on your path to success.

PART I

Create the Plan That Will Lead to
Your Success

CHAPTER ONE

Who Are You?

Are you not sure where you are headed in life? What do you envision for yourself? Are you really clear about what is important to you? Do you feel that your life is not moving in a positive direction? What do you want to accomplish in your life? What legacy will you leave?

The best way I know of to begin answering these questions is to develop a personal mission statement. While the mission statement will help you identify career goals, it goes much farther. It helps clarify your personal values and vision. It can help guide decisions in all aspects of your life.

Many companies of all sizes have corporate mission statements. These mission statements inform decisions and guide actions. They communicate to everyone, from suppliers and customers to employees, what the company is all about. When faced with an important decision, corporate leaders can refer to the mission statement. This allows them to make that decision in a manner that will support the overall goals of the company. Without a mission statement, it is easy to go astray and take actions that are counterproductive or even at odds with the organization's ultimate goals.

A personal mission statement functions in the same way. It provides direction, defines purpose, and guides your life choices. When you come to a crossroads in life, a mission statement allows you to chart the course that aligns with who you are.

It clarifies what you are about, who is the unique you and what is significant to you. It is always floating in the background and guiding your progress. It provides boundaries that guide actions and help make tough decisions.

Crafting a personal mission statement is a thoughtful process that will take time. I discovered that when I tried to complete the process in one sitting, I overlooked important elements. Work on the statement, then set it aside and let it percolate in your subconscious.

Return to the initial draft a few days later. You may have found that additional insights came to you that originally went undiscovered.

Let's get started on your personal mission statement. The process begins with a brainstorming session. The five steps outlined below will guide you through the progression of building a well thought out statement. Use the prompts in each step to write out a list of values, traits, talents, and aspirations. These lists will provide the background for crafting your mission statement.

Identify your core values

Think about what is significant in your life. Think of past successes and what made you proud. What have they been? Examples of personal successes could be that you completed a 5k run, you completed a craft project, or you helped with a successful school fundraiser. In your work, you may have come up with a creative solution for a problem, or you may have received positive recognition from your supervisor for something that you did. Begin by listing as many examples of these successes as you can think of.

Describe what makes you happy. Do you enjoy walking in a park? Do cultural attractions inspire you? Are you excited by a night of dining and dancing? Do you feel a sense of contentment when you are helping a child learn something new? Looking at the types of activities that bring you joy are key to understanding. Add these to your list.

Pinpoint your key personality traits

List the positive personal attributes that best describe you. What adjectives best represent your character. A list of your attributes may contain descriptors such as honest, thoughtful, generous, tenacious, creative, competent, nurturing, playful, careful, or competitive. Are you outgoing or reserved? Are you patient, sympathetic, skeptical, organized or disciplined?

If you are like me, you may want to ask others for feedback. I have found that I don't always give myself credit for my positive traits. By asking a trusted friend or relative, you may learn more about yourself than you realize.

Think about your strengths and talents

Make a list completing the statement "I am good at..." with as many words and phrases as you can think of. What have you received recognition or praise for? For example, "I am good at solving problems," or "I am able to explain complex ideas to others so they understand them."

This list can also benefit from feedback by others. Ask them what they think you are good at. You may be surprised. When I first completed this exercise, friends noted that I was very good at teaching people new things. I had never considered myself as a teacher or trainer until then.

Describe your aspirations

This is where you want to dream big. Think about where you want to go. Consider where you want to physically go, but also think about where you want to go in your mental and spiritual development. Don't judge your answers to this prompt. Let your imagination run free. In this exercise there are no constraints. For example, maybe you have always wanted to live in a foreign country, or maybe your favorite place is the home you grew up in. This is your list. Make it meaningful for you.

Ask yourself - what legacy do you want to leave?

Look at the previous lists and note what you want to accomplish in your life. What do you want friends and loved ones to remember about you? The answer to this prompt can become the foundation for mission statement. Your mission statement is more than just a set of goals. The answers you develop in this section will enable you to define your mission. Armed with the mission statement, you will begin to lay the groundwork for short-term and long-term goals that will guide you forward.

Write your mission statement

Keep the five lists you made handy as you write a rough draft. Keep it positive, and I have found it is most helpful if you keep it in the present tense. Make it concise. A good personal mission statement will be about one or two paragraphs.

Revisit your statement several times over the next couple of weeks and make any modifications that you want. Maybe you left something out of the first draft or maybe you want to remove something. You want to be comfortable that the end result describes you and your mission in life.

Your mission statement is not a static text chiseled in stone, it should be a living document. Your core values will rarely change over time. However, as you gain life experience, you may come to see things in a different light. How you interpret your personal values can change over time as you discover new things about yourself, find yourself in new situations, or take advantage of new opportunities.

* * *

Key Reminders

- Your mission statement should reflect your basic values.

- Don't expect to complete the mission statement in one sitting. It takes time.

- Make this <u>your</u> statement. Don't rely on others to tell you what your mission statement should be.

- Write down your mission statement.

- Regularly revisit your mission statement to keep yourself on track and energized.

CHAPTER TWO

Where Do You Want to Go?

Think of your personal mission statement as a compass. It points you toward a particular destination. It doesn't tell you how you will get there, however. That is where the next phase comes in. You need to develop a plan on how to achieve what you want in life and you do this by clearly refining and stating your goals.

Establishing goals is the next step in this process. A goal-setting exercise will provide the roadmap that you can follow. It will help you determine concrete steps that you can take to fulfill your personal mission. Research has shown that goal setting is a potent tool for helping us live the life we want to live and accomplish what we want to accomplish.

My own experience has shown me that just the act of setting goals will significantly increase the chances for success in every area of your life. When I rigorously applied the goal-setting process, I was able to achieve results in my personal and career life that went beyond what I thought I could accomplish. There have also been times in my life when I neglected the goal-setting process. As I look back, those were the times when I felt lost, not knowing what to do next.

As you work your way through the goal-setting technique that I will describe, don't set limits on yourself. You should develop a list of goal statements that will be as long as you need. There have been times in my life when my list has included 50 or more goals. Much of the magic of goal-setting is that your subconscious mind can offer powerful support in the process. Once you have written down your goals and sincerely believe that you can achieve them, you will begin moving toward them, even when you are not consciously aware that you are doing so.

Characteristics of an effective goal statement

Good goal statements answer three questions. They should describe (1) What you will accomplish, (2) When you will have accomplished it, and (3) Why you want to accomplish it. It may also be helpful to include the fourth W, where, if the goal is place-specific. Many goal-setting programs focus on the what and when, but I have found that adding why it is important adds a potent dimension to the goal statement.

Your goals must be clear and concise

To be effective, your goal statements have to have certain components. They have to be clear and precise. A goal statement such as "I want to lose weight" is too general. Statements like "I will lose ten pounds in the next three months" or "I will weigh XXX pounds by such and such a date" are more specific and offer a clear picture of what you want to accomplish.

Your goals must be meaningful

Your goals must be significant. They must be meaningful to you, and they must be your personal goals. That's why we begin the process with our mission statement. Your goals must align with your personal values. If you let other people, whether it is a partner, a friend or an employer, determine your goals, you diminish your chance for success.

Your goals must be practical and attainable

Goals have to be practical and attainable. There is nothing wrong with including expansive goals on your list. However, they still must be grounded in reality and you must be capable of attaining them. Your goals should not rely on other people for their attainment. It should be under your direct control. "My spouse will earn xxx dollars per year" relies on your spouse, rather than you, taking specific actions.

Your goals must be measurable

You have to have a way of knowing when you reach your goal. If your goal is that you want to be a better tennis player, it is impossible to assess your progress toward the goal. You should state the goal in terms of what you can see, hear or measure in some way. A measurable goal about your tennis skill could be something like "I will qualify to compete in my age-group tournament at the local tennis club."

Your goals must have a deadline

Without a specific deadline, there is no urgency for moving toward completion. The resolve that a deadline imparts can create a strong incentive for both your conscious and your subconscious mind. Without a timeline, your goal becomes "I will get around to it someday," and it is too easy to put off the actions you need to take in order to reach the goal.

Your goals must be written down

While you may have confidence that you will always be able to mentally keep track of your goals, a mental tracking system will only work if you have a few simple goals. Unwritten goals are merely hopes and dreams, they are not goals. Putting your goals down in a written document will give them a life of their own. They become real and tangible. They are easy to refer to, and it is easy to track your progress.

In my experience it actually works best when I take pen or pencil in hand. Rather than typing them on a keyboard, I physically write down my goals. There seems to be something about the physical act of writing that makes them more real, more palpable. If you want to type out a clean, legible version of your goals, I urge you to do that after you have written them out by hand.

Finally, I have found that it is very helpful to include the "why" in your goal statement. Why is attaining this goal important to you? What benefits will the attainment of this goal lead to? By attaching a "why" to every goal, you clarify the goal's importance. By doing this, you also make it clear what you will gain from attaining the goal.

In the next chapter, I will lead you on a step-by-step journey through the goal-setting process.

* * *

Key Reminders

- Your goals should be meaningful to you.

- Your goals should be practical and attainable.

- At the same time you goals should not be so easily attained that they limit personal development.

- Your goals should be clear and concise.

- Make sure you include the "whys" in your goal statements.

- Effective goal statements must be recorded in writing.

CHAPTER THREE

What Are Your Goals?

Now, it's time to dig into the details of the goal setting procedure. I recommend a logical progression to your process that begins large in scope and then moves down into the specifics. The goals you reveal and write out in this chapter will lay the groundwork for developing action steps. Action steps are the specific activities you will take that will lead to the accomplishment of your goals.

Let's begin your goal-setting session. Start by reviewing the personal mission statement you developed. You will want to keep this in mind as you work through the goal-setting session. Your goals should align with your mission in life. Without this alignment, you will find that achieving the goals you set will be difficult.

As you go through the goal-setting exercise, you may discover that you need to make modifications to your mission statement. That's okay as long as you are comfortable that the changes reflect who you are. If you discover that you are tempted to make dramatic changes to your personal mission statement, you may want to review Chapter One to make sure your changes truly reflect your values.

To provide a structure as you formulate your goals, you can think about the different aspects of your life as separate categories. The list below includes the major categories that you may want to consider. These categories are distinct, however there is also quite a bit of overlap.

> Health, fitness, and diet goals
> Work and career goals
> Relationship goals
> Quality of life, personal development, and social life goals
> Wealth and finance goals
> Spirituality goals

A goal in one of these areas may need a supporting goal in another area. For example, there is a strong relationship between work/career goals and wealth/finance goals. One definitely will impact the other. As you work through the exercise, you will probably find that some of the areas of your life are more important than others. It is also important to understand that you can't work on one area of your life and ignore the others. There has to be a balance.

Step One – Dream big

Begin the goal setting exercise by dreaming and brainstorming. List each of the categories of your life at the top of a separate sheet of paper. Again, I urge you to do this exercise by physically writing down your thoughts rather than typing them on a keyboard. Take one category at a time and give it some deep thought.

This is the time for quiet reflection. Do this exercise at a time when you will not be interrupted. Turn off your phone, shut down your computer, put a "do not disturb" sign on your door, or do whatever it takes so that you will have an uninterrupted session. Ideally, you will allot an hour or so for this part of the exercise. It is also important that you don't rush through it. Give your inner self the time to reveal your thoughts and desires.

At this point, you want to dream big. What do you really want? Write down everything that comes to mind. Make each list as long as it needs to be. This is not the time to be judgmental. Resist the urge to discard some of your dreams offhand because you don't think they are feasible. Have the confidence in your ability to accomplish whatever you want.

Step Two – Turn your dreams into goals

It's time to refine and prioritize the lists you made. Look at the "dream lists" you made in each area and begin to turn them into goal statements. Write out the statements into sentences beginning with

"I will be" or "I will have." Avoid terms like hope or wish. Make them positive sentences even though you will not have accomplished the goal yet.

The key to achievable goals it to make sure they are performance goals rather than outcome goals. Performance goals describe what you will do. These are based on actions that you will take. You have less control over outcome goals.

For instance, if your goal is to receive a promotion at work, there are a lot of factors beyond your control that may affect the outcome. Your company may go through a downturn and freeze all promotions, or you may get a new supervisor with different priorities than the previous one. So, focus on what you will do to put you in the best position for a promotion.

Both these scenarios happened to me during my corporate career. Each time, I was determined to focus on actions that I could control. I studied the organization and talked with my supervisor. I learned what positive actions I could take to support my supervisor's and the company's goals. Ultimately, in every case, I ended up exceeding my expectations.

Start with the long-term (five years or more)

As you look through your goal statement, you should give some thought to a time frame associated with each of them. You should determine which goals are ones that you would expect to attain in the near future and which ones may take longer. It is important to have some "dream big" goals. It may be three to five years or more before you can reasonably expect to attain these long-term goals. At the same time, some of the goals will be achievable in a shorter time.

Beginning with the goals you labeled as long-term, put each of them into a goal statement that has the characteristics that are described in Chapter Two (what you will accomplish and when you will accomplish it). Describing WHEN is just as important as saying WHAT you will do. Add WHY it is important to reach the goal (tie it back to your personal mission statement if you can).

Then create short-range goals

The next step is to develop short-term goals that support the long-term ones. Look at each of the long-term goals and think about what intermediate steps will lead to that goal. For example, if your goal is to be able to complete a marathon race five years from now, you might have a short-term goal of completing a 5K run in one year.

For each of your long-term goals, you should be able to come up with one or more short-term goal. Make sure you have a measure of success for every goal. How will you know when you have achieved it? Every time you have success with one of these short-term goals, you will be adding a dose of positive reinforcement that will keep you motivated.

As you develop these goals, you should also keep in mind the roadblocks that might pop up. What might keep you from achieving them? Do you need more education to reach the goals in your work and finance category?

For me, this was a big issue. My goal was to move from positions in corporate management into training and teaching. While I had a lot of experience, I determined that I was lacking in the formal education required for me to change careers. At that point, I went back to college. I was able to combine my practical experience with what I learned at the university and move into a teaching career.

Are procrastination, lack of confidence or difficulties with self-motivation areas that you struggle with? In my experience, having a strong goal-setting process and a specific action plan, I have been able to overcome my tendencies toward procrastination and keep myself motivated.

Add accountability

Once you've developed your list of goal statements, I recommend that you bring them out in the open. Share your goals with the appropriate people. Ideally, you have supportive people in your life who can cheer when you accomplish a goal, and they may even suggest actions you can take as you venture toward the goal. Sharing your goal with others will add an element of accountability.

* * *

Key Reminders

- Make sure that your goals are activities within your control.

- Write down the goals (you can type them but you should also physically write them).

- Write down the "whys." This validates that the goal is worth striving for.

- Go back and read your goals regularly but don't overdo it. A regular monthly or quarterly review cycle works well for most people.

- As you review your goals, visualize yourself achieving them. You might even want to write out a statement describing what success will look like.

CHAPTER FOUR

Where Are You Now?

Now it's time to do some self-assessment. Do you have the tools to accomplish your goals? When you thought about possible roadblocks, what did you discover? Think about what knowledge or skills your goals will require. In many cases, you will discover that you need additional resources to achieve the goal, like I did when I found I needed a higher college degree to transition into teaching.

In some areas, this may be obvious. Do you need to learn about accounting or finance in order to accomplish your work-related goals? Do you need to study up on nutrition so that you can reach a weight loss goal? Do you need to get a passport to attain a travel aspiration? Unless you set your goals too low, you will likely find that there is something that you can do or get that will be essential to your success.

Determine what the goal requires

Begin with your long-term goals. Look at them one at a time, and make a list of what knowledge, skills, and abilities are required to achieve the goals. During this first stage, you shouldn't concern yourself with whether or not you have what you need. Do some research, ask others for advice. You want to develop a comprehensive checklist of what is needed to complete the goal.

If you know someone who has achieved a goal similar to yours, connect with them to validate your list. If your goal is to attain a promotion, you may want to ask your supervisor to help you decide what areas you want to work on. If you are hoping to go into a new career field, it would be advantageous to interview someone who is already in that field. For my goal of transitioning from management positions to teaching, I reached out to people who were teaching at the types of institutions that I was interested in.

Review the gaps

Now, for each of the lists of goal requirements, evaluate what skills, abilities, and knowledge you currently have that are essential for reaching the goal. Then, look at what you still need in order to succeed. In some instances you will realize that you have all the knowledge and abilities you need. In other instances, you will see there are some gaps between what you need and what you have.

At this point, it is a good idea to think about your support network. Are there people in your life who can help you along this journey? Whether it is a partner, relative, friend or co-worker, it is helpful to have someone who you can talk with about this. A brainstorming session with someone you trust is very helpful for clarifying your thoughts.

Determine what actions you will take to address those weaknesses

Review the short-term goals associated with each of the long-term goals. You want to make sure that the short-term goals include attaining the knowledge and skills that will lead to the long-term goals. What areas do you want to develop further? Write down what, if anything, additional that you will need to accomplish the goal. For example, you may need additional education, skills, training, personal contacts, finances, or simply practice. Addressing these areas of weakness will become an important part of your goal attainment action plans. In addition to making plans that address your areas of weakness, you should incorporate actions that move you forward toward your goals.

Make an action plan to-do list

What actions are you going to take to move toward your goal? You need a specific written plan of action so you can begin moving forward. Write it out. In my experience, I've found that, if I don't write it down, it can easily slip off my radar.

I begin with a monthly plan. I write down all the actions that I plan to take in the next month that will drive me towards my goal. Maybe I want to find a workshop to help me understand my personal finances. I put "I will spend one hour researching personal finance workshops" on my monthly list. When I research topics such as that one, it is easy for me keep on looking for the ideal answer. So, the next item on my list would be "I will make a decision on which personal finance workshop I will attend by the end of this month."

Use positive statements

Note that my plan of action includes the "I will" statements that your goals have. By adding the "I will" statement, you are making a commitment to yourself that this is important. It may take some effort to force yourself to sit down each month and write out your plans. For me it was a struggle at the beginning, but it eventually became a habit. Now, I become frustrated when I don't have my list of actions to follow.

Break the plan into manageable segments

Armed with the monthly plan, you can break it down into weekly segments. What activities will you complete each week? Make sure that all your monthly to-do items are included somewhere on your weekly plans. If an activity isn't assigned to a particular week, it can easily be put off or forgotten.

For more structure and detail, you can break down the weekly lists into daily plans. However, for me, using the monthly and weekly lists works well. I have tried daily lists at times, but the daily lists created extra work, and they didn't seem to make a difference in my goal accomplishment. Make daily lists if you think you need them to stay on track, but you may find monthly and weekly will work just fine.

* * *

Key Reminders

- To make your goals a reality, you need to develop a plan of action.

- Determine what skills and abilities you need to hone; and think about new skills you will need to learn in order to attain your goals.

- Don't try to accomplish everything at once. Break the plan into manageable segments.

- Use positive "I will" statements.

CHAPTER FIVE

Take Action

Okay, you've set your goals and developed your action plans. The next step may be the hardest for many people. It is time to take action and move forward. There may be many reasons why you haven't already reached your goals. In my experience, most of the reasons I gave myself for not moving forward on my plan were excuses rather than valid reasons. The roadblocks in my way were usually of my own making.

Stay focused

Keep your personal action plans out in the open. Post them on your computer, tape them to your desk, or position them somewhere so they are openly visible. It is impossible for me to ignore my list of action items when I have them staring me in the face. If your space at work isn't conducive to an open display, make sure you keep them visible at home. When I had activities that I felt were really important but I couldn't post them at work (such as researching a new career), I posted the action items on my bathroom mirror.

I have found that the key to accomplishing your goals is straightforward. As the slogan for a large apparel company implores, the only way to move forward is to just do what needs to be done. Your subconscious mind is naturally a goal-seeking device. It wants to help you succeed. You have to keep reminding it about your goals so that it can continue directing you toward your goal even when your conscious mind has doubts.

Stay motivated

It all sounds so easy. Make a plan. Then just go out and do it. While this is a simple strategy, it is not always easy to follow through. A lot of things can derail your progress. So, you need to prepare yourself for the inevitable days and weeks when following the plan is a difficult chore. You may be tempted just to give up on the action plan, and in doing so, give up on the goal.

Whatever your long-term goals are, working towards them will probably take you out of your comfort zone. You will have to do some things that you have never tried before. If your goals were easy to accomplish, you would have already accomplished them, and you would be living your dream life.

When I run into a difficult period, I go back to my original goal statements. I review the "why" statements. Why was achieving this goal so important that I made it a goal in the first place? Striving for a goal is an indication that you are not completely satisfied with the way things are now. Reviewing why you want to make a change will re-emphasize the importance of the goal.

Create early wins

Another tactic is to aim for some early wins. It is always a good idea to structure your action plans so that some of the initial activities will be relatively easy to accomplish. Once you have accomplished some of your initial action items, you can move on to ones that may be harder or take more time.

When I set a goal to lose weight, one of the actions I decided to undertake was to begin a daily aerobic exercise. My knees do not appreciate it when I run, so I decided on an aerobic walking program.

My goal was to walk forty-five minutes every day, but I realized that I wouldn't be able to keep up with the program if I started out with a forty-five-minute walk on the first day. I began with fifteen minutes a day. Over a couple months, I gradually extended it until I was at forty-five minutes.

The other issue I encountered on my walking program is that I occasionally missed a day of walking for one reason or another. My plan was to walk every day, and when I first missed a day of walking

I became frustrated with myself. I came to realize that I could give myself permission to miss a day occasionally because it would not derail my progress. What would derail my progress was to use that as an excuse to give up on the goal.

Unless you take action to realize them, your goals are nothing more than hopes. Relying on the hope that something will happen is futile because it means that you no longer control the outcome. You relinquish the power of the situation to other factors. The purpose of setting goals and developing action plans is to take control of your situation. For me, the most motivational aspect of a comprehensive goal-setting process is that I can gain control over my situation. I can take positive steps to make a change. To me that is a very powerful feeling.

Key Reminders

- Make you action plans conspicuous. Display them where you can regularly see them.

- Keep yourself motivated by creating early wins, and keep the "why" statements at the top of your mind.

- Be prepared for setbacks. They will occur but they can be temporary if you keep your eyes on the goal.

CHAPTER SIX

Close the Feedback Loop

I once aspired to become a scientist, so I enrolled as an undergraduate in a university known for its engineering program. While I eventually learned that a science or engineering career didn't excite me, I learned a lot about how the world works from that engineering program. An important concept that I remember from those days is the idea of a positive feedback loop. While it is a valuable process in engineering, I have found that the feedback loop is also a strong factor in our personal success.

When you create a positive feedback loop, you will amplify your actions in a constructive way. When you take a step toward your goal and recognize the results that you achieve, you set the feedback process in motion. Recognizing the results encourages you to take the next action and, if necessary, make adjustments. As you continue to review the results of your actions, you take additional steps. The process builds on itself.

Create your feedback loop

How do we harness the power of the feedback loop? We establish a regular review schedule. We measure the results of the actions we took. We determine what effect those results had by asking ourselves if the actions achieved what we had intended. We decide on the next action. If everything is going as we planned, we move on to the next task in our action plan. If we notice a problem, we make adjustments to our action plan.

When I set a goal to lose weight, I took a two pronged approach to the issue. I adjusted my calorie intake and I began an exercise program. One of the first steps in my action plan was to track on a chart the number of calories I was eating every day. Every morning I would add up how many calories I consumed the previous day. When my previous day was over my daily calorie limit, I would cut back for a day. When I was on track the previous day, I would be encouraged to keep it up. Utilizing the feedback loop kept me on track for my goal. Eventually, I found that I didn't need to keep tracking my calories any longer. Keeping the calorie count in the desired range became a habit.

Develop a review schedule

The lesson here is that it is essential to establish a regular review schedule. I recommend that you conduct a weekly review session at a minimum. Once a week you should assess the progress on your action plans. Think about what effect they had. Did you make progress? Do you need to make any adjustments? Then, set up a plan for the coming week.

You might find it helpful to do a quick daily review throughout the week, but that will depend on what action steps you have built into your plan. Some people set up a daily progress calendar. For me, daily tracking has been extremely useful when I started out on a new goal. However, daily tracking eventually became too time consuming for me and was less beneficial as time went on. Do a daily review if it helps you maintain momentum, but I believe that a weekly review is the critical part of the process.

You also want to include a more long-term review process. Monthly, or every three month, check-ins will be beneficial. I have found an annual review the ideal time to take a look at the overall progress toward the goals in all my life categories. You should determine an evaluation schedule that works for you. Your reviews should be often enough so that you will know if you are on track, but they should not be so often that they become a chore.

Share your results if it will help

The other question you have to answer is whether you should share your results with someone else or keep them to yourself. I have found that by enlisting a supportive partner in the process, it is easier for me to stay on track. Pick a partner who truly wants to help you succeed. You might want to enlist someone who will just listen as you describe your results. I find that helpful because by explaining my results to someone else, I clarify them in my own mind. If you allow your partner to provide criticism, make sure it is in the form of positive suggestions. A negative partner can easily derail the progress you are making.

When you do your evaluation, you should ask yourself the following questions. Did I achieve the results I had planned to achieve? What is working? If I didn't achieve the planned results, are there additional resources I need? What plans do I need to re-adjust?

As you review the progress toward your goals, it is important that you recognize your accomplishments. Reward yourself when you accomplish a milestone. The celebration doesn't have to be extravagant. Whether it is a special dinner out to celebrate an accomplishment at work or a small gift you buy for yourself to celebrate hitting a weight-loss goal, the point is you are recognizing your success.

Rewards are an important part of the positive feedback loop. You may even set up a reward system when you first establish your goals. Recognizing and rewarding your accomplishments will be a strong motivator to keep you on track.

Use the feedback

Ask yourself these questions when you do your review. They are especially helpful during the annual review. What lessons did you learn from the goals you achieved? Was the goal easily reached? Perhaps the next goal needs to be harder if it was too easily reached.

If you don't have some goals that stretch your abilities, review the original goal-setting session. How do your activities align with your personal mission statement and move you toward accomplishing your dreams? If you accomplished a goal but it took more time than you planned, I recommend you consider adjusting your time goals.

An important part of the review process is to learn from the goals you are not achieving. Was the goal unrealistic? Did you not try hard enough? Were the skills or knowledge inadequate? If you consistently fail to achieve a particular goal, you may want to reassess how important it is for you to reach the goal.

Try to think about why you are missing the goal. Is it not as important as you originally thought? Is it not attainable? Do you need to re-set your short-term goals? Do you need additional tools (knowledge, skills, or abilities)?

The feedback loop is an essential element of success. You have to continually review and revise in order to make progress. If you felt your dreams were important enough to turn them into goals, then you owe it to yourself to do everything you can to work toward those goals.

* * *

Key Reminders

- Track your progress toward your goals.

- You can publicly share your goals to give them more significance.

- Enlist a trusted accountability partner to keep on track.

- Continually make course corrections as you progress.

PART II

Recognize and Overcome the Obstacles to Your Success

CHAPTER SEVEN

Stay Motivated – Keep Your Progress Going

If you followed the first part of the book, you now have a personal mission statement, a set of goals, and the action plans to lead you forward. Great work! You are on your way. Once you have developed the plan and taken steps toward realization of your goals, your next challenge is to keep the progress going.

It's often a lot easier to plan out the action than to keep moving forward. There is work involved, and you may be stepping out of your comfort zone. Many people make New Year's resolutions, only to abandon those resolutions in a few months. The way to building a successful life is to keep moving forward and not give up.

While you may have a supportive team to cheer you on, and this helps, you need to understand that the motivation to reach your goals has to come from you. No one else has as much to gain from your actions as you do.

Accept the slumps

The first thing you have to understand is that there will be slumps. Roadblocks will appear just as you think everything is going along smoothly. Accept that. There are times when I step on the scale and find that I have gained weight even though I was following my diet and exercise regime. That can be discouraging, but I have learned that if I use that weight gain as an excuse to give up on my diet and exercise, I will never reach my target weight. I have to keep proceeding on my plan.

It is important that you realize that mistakes and setbacks will happen. If you understand that they are just part of the process, you can do what is necessary to power through that setback or make a course correction. You have to keep working on your plan even when it seems you are not making any progress.

There will also be times when things go better than you were expecting. Many times in my work career, the promotions I received were unexpected. At times, the opportunities arose were well beyond my expectations for that stage in my career growth. Don't expect a straight line growth as you move toward your goals. Keep in mind, however, that the only thing that will completely derail your progress is if you stop trying.

Take positive action

Staying motivated and on track isn't always easy. Over the years, I have found that there are actions you can take that will help you stay motivated and keep you moving forward. Your personal mission statement is a key to keeping on track. Post it where you can see it every day so that you are continually reminded about your purpose in life. It is easy to get caught up in the minutiae of everyday life and lose track of the larger picture, so keep referring back to your mission statement.

For many people, visualization is a strong motivator. Take a quiet time, close your eyes and visualize what life will be like when you reach your goals. Make a mental image in your mind of performing an action. Envision what will happen and how you will feel when you reach the goal. The more detailed the visualization is, the more influence it will have on your subconscious mind. This technique is often used in sports, such as a basketball player visualizing the ball going through the hoop before shooting the ball.

A technique I use at times when I feel that I am not achieving the results I expected is what I call the "just do something" method. I tell myself that I need to take one action. It can be a small step but it will get you moving again. When I come to a point in my writing when I think I am stuck, I tell myself to sit down and write one paragraph. Generally when I sit down to write a paragraph, I find that the words begin to flow and I will have written a page without realizing it. One small action can help you break out of a slump.

Reward yourself

Keep yourself motivated with a reward system. As you track your progress, think about mileposts along your path that you can celebrate. You can reward yourself for completing certain actions, for instance recognizing when you have exercised for thirty days in a row or when you complete a project at work. You can also reward yourself for accomplishments, such as when you complete an online course. Set up a reward system that combines recognition for taking actions and for accomplishments.

One of the most powerful techniques that propels me toward my goals is keeping a positive mindset. It is easy to stay positive when you are cruising along, meeting your interim goals, and seeing the results of your actions. It is more challenging to stay positive when you are not making progress, but that is when a positive mindset is even more important.

You must remind yourself that, when you established your goals and action plans, you gave thought to coming up with goals that were realistic and achievable. One important key is to surround yourself with positive, supportive people whenever possible. Identify those friends and relatives who will offer positive support and try to limit your exposure to people who don't offer support. You want honest feedback, however it should be feedback from people who offer support.

The strongest motivator I have in my endeavors has been to just take an action. Every action I take toward my goal provides the impetus to take one more action. You will build your future one step at a time and, to ensure that future comes, you need to keep taking that next step.

* * *

Key Reminders

- Keep in mind there will be setbacks. Make them temporary and keep moving forward.

- Keep on track by focusing on the next positive action you will take.

- Give yourself positive feedback with rewards as you make progress on your goals.

CHAPTER EIGHT

Build Your Confidence

One of the biggest roadblocks I have faced in my work life and in my personal life, and still face at times, is lack of confidence. The nagging questions always hang around in the back of my mind. Can I really accomplish this? What if these actions don't help me realize my goals? What if I don't succeed? I think everyone struggles with this to some degree.

I imagine that most of the people I have worked with over the years would find it hard to believe that I was struggling with self-confidence. I was able to project an air of confidence, but inside I felt I was putting on an act. Even when things were not going well, I could act as if I had confidence in my actions. I believe that one of the keys to my many successes in the workplace has been my ability to keep a calm, steady, confident demeanor even when I was under tremendous stress.

Recognize your successes

Confidence comes from recognizing your abilities and taking action even in difficult circumstances. Nothing builds self-confidence better than success. Keep track of your successes. When you review the progress toward your goals, you should pay particular attention to what went right. We often gloss over our accomplishments and focus on the things that went wrong. While you want to recognize the areas where improvement is needed, it is even more important to celebrate what went right.

When you review the progress you are making toward your goals, make a list of what you did that was successful. It is a good idea to keep a written list of these accomplishments so you can refer back to them. Review this list of accomplishments often, and they will exert a positive influence on your subconscious mind when you are faced with a challenging situation.

Take concrete actions

Learn something new. If your lack of confidence is rooted in a feeling that you don't know how to be successful, you need to address that. Take a class to learn about the areas where your knowledge is lacking. For example, if you want to become better with finance, take a math class or an accounting course at a local community college. Educational resources are available in nearly every community. If you can't find what you need locally, check out online courses. You can find a course about any topic online.

Change a habit. Make it a simple, straightforward change. Set your alarm to wake you ten minutes earlier and use that ten minutes to meditate. Write down a grocery list before you go shopping. Read for ten minutes a day. Choose something small that you know you can do. Continue the new activity for a month.

Reach out of your comfort zone

Identify actions that will take you out of your comfort zone. It can be a bit scary to take on something that you are wary of, but take that step. Look at areas of your job that make you uncomfortable and take them on. Volunteer for a special project that will stretch your abilities. I have done this many times throughout my career, and I feel it has done the most to boost my self-confidence.

When I left a successful career at an educational institution, I thought about continuing my teaching career at another local institution. Instead, I opted to look for an opportunity to work in a foreign country. While it was a job I could do, moving to another country was intimidating. I was nervous at first, but I learned that I could become successful in this new situation.

You can also identify ways to reach out of your comfort zone in your non-work life. For example, I would venture to guess that most people are intimidated by speaking in public. Becoming comfortable talking in front of groups can be a real boost to their overall confidence. There are clubs, such as the Toastmasters, in every community that offer the opportunity to become skilled at public speaking.

Use positive self-talk

How you talk to yourself can have a strong influence on how confident you are. It may be hard at times to tell yourself you can do something when you are unsure if you can, but keep telling yourself you will be successful and your odds for success increase. Listen to your internal voice and pay attention to the times when negative thoughts arise. When those negative thoughts arise, you have to attack them with a positive response. When you think "I can't do this," change it to "I will do this."

Resist the urge to compare yourself with others.

Every person has a set of unique skills and abilities. When you compare yourself to others, you lose sight of what you are good at. Learn what your strengths are and use them to your advantage. Learn what areas you want to work on and take action.

The struggle with self-confidence is a struggle that all of us have to some degree. Accept that this is an area that requires constant attention. I can assure you that the people you encounter in your life who appear to be supremely confident also have moments of self-doubt. Confidence is not a genetic trait that is unchangeable, it is an attitude that can be changed.

* * *

Key Reminders

- Build confidence by keeping a focus on your successes.

- Keep on learning.

- Look for opportunities to move out of your comfort zone.

- Attack negative self-talk with positive affirmations.

- Keep focused on what you are doing, not what others are doing.

CHAPTER NINE

Overcome the "What ifs"

When you attempt to move forward on a bold plan, do you sometimes get a feeling of dread? What if it doesn't work? What if I don't succeed? What if it is more work than I thought it would be? What if my boss says no? What if I have to give up something that I am comfortable doing?

Those feelings are certainly familiar to me. As we go forward through life, especially when we embark on new endeavors, fears naturally crop up in our mind. The fears can manifest themselves in many forms. Fear of failure, fear of success, fear of rejection, and fear of discomfort are common emotions that we must deal with. Fear can be a resilient enemy to your progress.

These emotions can surface in a variety of ways. The butterflies in your stomach as you are about to give a presentation and the anxiety you feel when you take on new responsibilities are signs that this is happening. Fear is a potent force that can have wide-ranging effects. The effects range from giving you a feeling of mild discomfort to causing you to give up on your goals.

Learn to recognize the fears

The key to successfully overcoming these fears is to understand that they are natural and to prepare for them. You will never be able to completely vanquish those fears but, by taking them head-on, you can minimize their effect on your performance and the outcomes you strive to attain.

When your fears crop up, acknowledge them. Write them down. Then examine the facts objectively and write down responses to them. Yes, it's true that the worst case scenario may happen if you fail to reach your goals but, in most cases the likelihood of that happening is quite small. Often, the worst case scenario is that you will be no worse off after working on your action plan than you were before you began. Turn that fearful thought in your mind around so it becomes, "I definitely will not reach my goals if I don't take steps toward achieving them."

When you have a setback, which is inevitable, learn from it. Failures are learning opportunities that allow us to make course corrections as we proceed. The fear is natural but you can take control of your fear and turn it into a positive emotion.

Keep the end in sight

If your inner voice keeps telling you that this process is harder than you thought it would be, concede to yourself that it may be hard work. Instead of focusing on the work that you have to do to reach your goals, keep focused on the end results. Yes, that accounting class at the local community college may be hard work, but it will be worth the effort when it helps you get a promotion or supports your freelance business. If the actions you need to take were all easy for you to do, you would have already achieved your goals. It will take hard work, and it will be uncomfortable at times.

Being a good salesperson has never been easy for me. I do a good job explaining the features and benefits of what I am selling but, when it comes to asking for the sale, a fear of rejection always finds its way into my subconscious. "What if they say no?" "Maybe they won't like me if I push too hard." I only became successful when I realized that I cannot control anyone's reactions to me. They will think what they will think. I began to accept the fact that some people will say no. I came to understand that I was a successful person no matter what other people thought or how they reacted to me.

Fear arises in many different forms. Be prepared for it and don't let it hinder your progress. When I find myself fighting off fear, I go back and review my personal mission statement. I review the "whys" that I wrote down when I developed my goals. You have to keep remembering why you have undertaken this journey and why the outcomes will be worth the struggles.

Ultimately, you have to work through the fears. Yes, they will continue to crop up and try to sabotage your progress. Yes, things will be hard and uncomfortable. The only time fear wins is when you give up and walk away from your dreams. You can't let that happen.

* * *

Key Reminders

- Realize that fears and self-doubt are natural and acknowledge them when they occur.

- Stay focused on your progress and keep the end goals in sight.

- Review your mission statement to maintain focus on what is important.

CHAPTER TEN

Beat Procrastination

Okay, you have a plan, and you know what you need to do to achieve your goals, but you just can't seem to get around to working on the plan. Putting an important task off by filling your time with minor busywork, yielding to distractions, or waiting for the right time to begin are the tell-tale signs of procrastination. If you are postponing an important action for a good reason, that may be a valuable part of the process. However, putting actions off continually or avoiding doing something because it may be unpleasant can derail your progress before you start.

Generally, I am fully aware that I am procrastinating when I am in that state. For me, procrastination causes a great deal of internal stress. I know I should begin the task but I find all kinds of excuses to keep from moving forward. When you find yourself procrastinating, begin by asking yourself why you are procrastinating. Is the task boring or does it lack meaning for you? Are you not sure what the next task is that you should do, or is it difficult?

Since the actions we are talking about are the steps to meet your life goals and fulfill your personal mission statement, you can begin defeating procrastination by reviewing why you embarked on this path to begin with. Think about your self-talk about the topic. Changing your inner dialogue from "I have to" to "I choose to because..." will emphasize the reasons for moving ahead. Here are strategies to break out of the procrastination rut.

Focus on beginning

The whole process may feel daunting. This is especially true when we embark on a journey of personal change. There are so many steps that you need to take in order to reach your goals that you wonder if you will ever make it through your journey to a more successful life. Combat this apprehension by focusing on starting. What is the first action you need to take? If you want to get into physical condition so that you can complete a 5K run, tell yourself "today I will begin by running for fifteen minutes."

Find an accountability partner

I absolutely hate letting others down. When I make a commitment to someone else, I do everything I can to keep that commitment. I use the same process to keep on track and avoid procrastinating. Share your goals with someone you trust. I share my plans with my spouse and family members, and that drives me to complete the tasks. I don't need to ask for their feedback or cheerleading, it is enough that I have made my intentions public. Make sure the people you share this with have a positive attitude toward your goals. You don't want a naysayer to disrupt your progress.

Just get started

Commit to yourself that you will do something every day to work on your action plans. If the next action step seems intimidating, break it into smaller activities and begin work on one of those. A technique I use is to tackle the least pleasant task first. Once that is done, the more enjoyable tasks are easier to work on. You may want to revisit the action plans you made to achieve your life goals and determine which ones are the most intimidating. Work on them first.

Remove distractions

When I am mired in a period of procrastination, I become distracted easily. Whether it is email, social media, or phone calls, anything that interrupts my progress can lead to a period of procrastination. To break out of a procrastination cycle, I need to shut out those disruptions. Think about what distractions you are drawn to and remove them while you work. Your emails will still be there after you have spent an hour working on your plan of action. Your social media friends will not miss you if you tune them out for a while.

Procrastination can rear its head up anytime in the process. It may stop you from beginning a project, or it may slow down your progress in the middle of the action. The key to overcoming it is to recognize that you are procrastinating, think about why you are procrastinating, and then take purposeful steps to begin moving forward.

* * *

Key Reminders

- Take it one step at a time.

- When you feel stuck, take one action that will move you forward.

- Recruit a partner to help you stay on track.

- Eliminate distractions as much as possible.

CHAPTER ELEVEN

Make Time to Achieve Success

A major roadblock for many people is carving out time when you have a busy schedule. If you work full time, it may seem hard to find those extra hours to work on your goals. However, the reality of the situation is that, unless you make the time, you will never achieve the success you deserve. You have spent the time creating the plan to reach your goals and to fulfill your personal mission in life. Continue the progress by using your time wisely.

Yes, it is often hard to make time to work on personal goals when you have a busy life. I know the feeling. I was working in a full-time job that demanded my total focus when I decided that the only way I could move forward on my path was to begin study in a graduate program. Working full time, attending class as a full-time student, and making time to study was difficult, but I managed it. If I can do it, so can you. You have to make it a priority to use your time wisely.

Conduct a time audit

When I began my graduate program, I quickly learned strategies that helped me capture the time that I needed to juggle everything in my life. The first step is to audit your time. Keep a written journal for one full week (a full seven-day week). Divide the day into blocks of thirty minutes or an hour, and write down what you are doing throughout the day. At the end of the seven days, review what activities you spent time on. Do you notice some blocks of time that were not very productive?

Over the course of my career, I have returned to this journaling exercise on several occasions and, every time I did it, I was able to make room for additional personal-growth activities. I was always surprised at how time wasters always crept back into my schedule.

Create extra time

You may want to consider creating extra time for yourself. Determine to get out of bed a half hour earlier every day to work on your action plans. Or, take thirty minutes at night before going to bed. Over a month's time, capturing an extra thirty minutes a day will add up to a substantial amount of time.

Several years ago, I began walking to improve my health. I was determined to walk at least forty-five minutes a day but, with a full-time job I wasn't sure where I would find the time. When I looked at how I was spending my time, I realized that I watched television for more than an hour every night. When I thought about it, I decided that walking to improve my health was more important to me than watching television, and I began an evening walking program.

Use your commuting time effectively. At times in my career, I was commuting by car for about forty-five minutes each way. I found that listening to audio books was a simple way to use that commute for personal enrichment. When I was in graduate school, I had switched to public transportation, and I was able to do the reading for my studies as I rode the bus.

Determine to use your weekend productively. You may be able to set aside time to work on your more time-consuming projects. You should also make it a priority to schedule in some rest and relaxation time on the weekend. Taking the time to recharge will allow you to be more productive when you are working toward your goals.

Make a daily task list

May a daily to-do list. Write down what you want to accomplish, and also write down the times during the day that you are going to work on your personal success. Block off uninterrupted time when you can really focus. If you can't set aside a large block of time, then you may be able to find several shorter intervals that you can put to effective use.

To find time for working on your goals, you may need to consider reducing the time commitments that are currently on your schedule. Consider cutting out one activity, like I did when I cut out watching television at night. You might also consider reducing your social activities for a while. You may have to say "no" to requests from friends and family members.

Negotiate for time

Consider negotiating for time. When I was studying, I negotiated with my supervisor to adjust my work schedule. I was able to block out some times during the work day to leave work and attend class. I committed to continue to meet all my work responsibilities by working later on other days.

When I was manager of a department, I worked out an agreement with one of my employees that she would work four ten-hour days so she could have one day a week off to attend school. Can you work out an arrangement like that? Think about other ways to negotiate for extra time. Can you negotiate a chore-sharing arrangement with your partner that will allow you to schedule times to work on your goals?

Don't let time constraints become an excuse for not moving forward toward your goals. It may take some thought, and you may have to be creative about it, but the time is there for you to use. You have to make it a priority to work on your success plan.

* * *

Key Reminders

- Review how you currently are using your time.

- Find ways to carve out small chunks of time to work on your action steps.

- Use a daily to-do list to keep on track.

- Look for ways to negotiate extra time to work on your goals.

THIS IS THE BEGINNING

You Can Do It

What does success in life mean to you? What do you want to get out of the time you spend on this earth? How are you going to achieve the outcomes you want to happen? What steps do you need to take? Each of us has our own unique set of answers to those questions.

After following the plan I describe in this book, you have now developed a clearer picture of what being you is all about. You have mapped out a plan to move forward in building a successful life and achieving your goals. I firmly believe that each of us have the capacity to achieve our goals.

The road you take on this journey will be bumpy. Obstacles will arise. The obstacles I described are lurking in and around all of us. There will also be new, and unforeseen, obstacles. Don't let that stop you.

There have been times in my life when it felt like the world was collapsing. I have been fired from a job, another job was eliminated by my organization's restructuring, I had to abandon an educational program just before I was about to complete it. I have had my share of setbacks in my personal life. But, I am proud say that I never gave up.

I kept going back to my personal mission. That has been my compass in life. Decades ago, I discovered the writings of the painter Vincent Van Gogh. The letters he wrote to his brother are often full of anguish, but many are inspirational. One quote I remember from him is "Success is sometimes the outcome of a whole string of failures." Don't let a setback stop you from trying.

At other times in my life, good things happened that I wasn't expecting. A promotion was offered to me out of the blue. A new career path opened up that I would never have planned for.

If you drift along without a plan, success in whatever way you define it, will be difficult to achieve. When you make a plan, work on that plan, and if you are prepared to tackle the difficulties that arise, you can be successful.

* * *

Key reminders

- Your mission statement, goals and action plans are powerful tools. Without them, success will be much harder to achieve.

- You will determine your outcomes. Just take the next step.

- Remember setbacks will occur. Vow to keep moving forward.

- Review your personal mission statement when you are in doubt about the next step.